Stepping Stones of Faith

Exciting
Lessons
to Help
Preschool
Children
Build
Faith

Anita
Edlund

Abingdon Press

Nashville

Stepping Stones of Faith:

Exciting Lessons to Help Preschool Children Build Faith

ISBN 978-0-687-64720-0

08 09 10 11 12 13 14 15 16 17—10 9 8 7 6 5 4 3 2 1

MANUFACTURED IN THE UNITED STATES OF AMERICA

Stepping Stones of Faith:
Table of Contents

DEDICATION

A special thanks to my friend, Ginger, whose encouragement gave my ideas wings to fly.
—Anita Edlund

STEPPING STONES OF FAITH
Introduction

Preschoolers are just beginning to learn about the world around them. What better time than now to instill in their minds some spiritual truths as well? There are many positive attributes of God that children of this age are capable of learning. Through *Stepping Stones of Faith* teachers are given ways to teach some of these concepts to the younger child.

There are twelve lessons in this book. Some are from the Old Testament and some are from the New Testament. Each lesson is a "stepping stone" to help build a child's belief in God and about God. Included in these lessons are crafts, games, snack ideas, songs, prayers, and ways the teacher can teach these truths to the children as they "step into the Bible and into faith" together.

Some of the stepping stones of faith in this material are: *God Loves Me, God Made the World & God Made Me, God Is Always With Me, God Understands My Feelings, God Will Listen When I Pray,* and *God Is Good.*

STEPPING STONES OF FAITH:

These lessons have been written so they could appear in the book in any order and can be used by the teacher in any order.

GOD LOVES ME

"Jesus Blesses the Children"
Mark 10:13-16

"Think how much the Father loves us. He loves us so much that he lets us be called his children."
(1 John 3:1, CEV)

GOD CARES ABOUT ALL OF ME

"The Birds and the Flowers"
Matthew 6:25-33

"God cares for you."
(1 Peter 5:7, CEV)

GOD UNDERSTANDS MY FEELINGS

"The Beatitudes"
Matthew 5:1-12

"Our LORD is great and powerful! He understands everything."
(Psalm 147:5, CEV)

GOD IS ALWAYS WITH ME

"David and Goliath"
1 Samuel 17:12-49

"Wherever you go, I will watch over you."
(Genesis 28:15, CEV)

GOD WILL HELP ME WHEN I AM AFRAID

"Daniel in the Lions' Den"
Daniel 6:1-27

"The LORD is on my side, and I am not afraid of what others can do to me."
(Psalm 118:6, CEV)

GOD WILL LISTEN WHEN I PRAY

"Jonah and the Big Fish"
Jonah 1:1–3:3

"The Lord watches over everyone who obeys him, and he listens to their prayers."
(1 Peter 3:12, CEV)

GOD LIKES TO BE PRAISED

"David Praises God"
2 Samuel 22:1-4;
Psalms 148, 150

"The LORD is great and deserves our greatest praise!"
(Psalm 96:4, CEV)

GOD WANTS ME TO HELP OTHER PEOPLE

"A Boy Helps Jesus"
John 6:1-14

"We should help people whenever we can."
(Galatians 6:10, CEV)

GOD KEEPS PROMISES

"Baby Jesus Is Born"
Matthew 1:18–2:11

"I will always keep the promise I have made to you ... because I am your God."
(Genesis 17:7, CEV)

GOD MADE THE WORLD & GOD MADE ME

"Creation"
Genesis 1:1–2:22;
Psalm 119:73

"You created me and put me together."
(Psalm 119:73, CEV)

GOD IS GOOD

"Hannah Has a Baby"
1 Samuel 1:6-20; 2:18-21

"Shout praises to the LORD! He is good to us, and his love never fails."

(Psalm 107:1, CEV)

GOD WILL NEVER STOP LOVING ME

"The Forgiving Father"
Luke 15:11-24

"O give thanks to the God of heaven, for his steadfast love endures forever."

(Psalm 136:26, NRSV)

6

STEPPING STONES OF FAITH:
GOD LOVES ME

"Think how much the Father loves us. He loves us so much that he lets us be called his children." (1 John 3:1, CEV)

STEPPING INTO THE BIBLE:
Jesus Blesses the Children
(Mark 10:13-16)

Before telling the story, red construction paper and a pair of scissors will be needed. Fold the paper in half. As you tell the story, cut out a large half heart on the folded edge. Leave the heart folded in half. Move in about ¼ inch and cut another half heart along that folded edge. Let the larger heart drop to the floor. It will actually be an outline of a heart. Keep the smaller heart in your hand. Continue cutting smaller and smaller hearts from this one sheet of paper as the story is told until there are enough hearts on the floor for each child to have one when the story is finished. If the group is large, more than one sheet of paper may be required.

Say: Many people wanted to see Jesus. Mommies wanted to see Jesus. Daddies wanted to see Jesus. They even brought their children to see Jesus. What a happy day this was!

Jesus had his helpers with him. When they saw all the people coming, they said to them, "Go away! Stop bothering Jesus." This was not a happy day now.

Jesus heard what his helpers told the people. Jesus did not like what they said. Jesus told his helpers, "Don't stop them. Let the children come to me." This was a happy day after all!

The children saw Jesus that day. Jesus took them in his arms and blessed them. Jesus loved the children. The children loved Jesus. Pick up all the hearts that were cut while the story was being told. Give one to each child. When handing the heart to the child, **say: Jesus loves you,** [Child's name].

CRAFTS:
Handprint Heart

Fold red construction paper in half like a book. On the folded edge, cut out half of a large heart. Open the paper to use the outside part. Save the red heart for another craft. Glue the red "frame" on top of white paper so that the edges are even. The child will make red handprints inside the heart. To make the handprint, the child can either dip a hand in a shallow pan containing paint and then place it on the paper or paint one hand using a brush and place that hand inside the heart. Have the child make one handprint leaning toward the left and one leaning toward the right. Let the palms of the two handprints overlap at the bottom of the heart. With a marker, write "God" at the top left of the red paper. At the bottom right of the red paper, write the child's name so that it now reads "God loves [Child's name]."

Handprint Heart Craft Supplies:

red construction paper

scissors

white paper

glue

red paint

shallow pan or paintbrush

hand-cleaning supplies

black marker

God ♥ Mary!

(red cut-out heart paper overlaps white paper

child's handprints done with red paint

A Happy Heart

Each child needs two large paper hearts and four smaller paper hearts to make a heart person. One large heart will be the face. Have the child draw a happy face on it. Use red, pink, or white chenille stems cut in shorter lengths to make the arms and legs. Attach two lengths to the sides of the large heart for arms and two pieces to the bottom for legs. Tape a small heart on the end of each piece for hands and feet. On the other large heart, write "God [heart] me!" You can draw a heart or let a child put a heart sticker there. Now glue that heart to the back of the face. Using chenille stems allows the child to bend the arms and legs in different positions. Remind the children that God loves each one of us. What a happy thing to know!

Snacks:
Jiggly Wiggly Hearts

Put gelatin in a bowl and add boiling water. Stir until the gelatin is dissolved. Spray a 9" x 13" pan lightly with cooking spray. This will make removing the gelatin easier. Now pour the gelatin into the pan and chill for three hours. (The gelatin may be firm after just one hour, but it will be harder to remove the shapes from the dish.) When it is time to cut the gelatin into hearts, dip the bottom of the pan in warm water for about 15 seconds to loosen the gelatin. Cut the gelatin with a heart-shaped cookie cutter. Make sure that it goes all the way through the gelatin. Lift the red hearts from the pan with an index finger or a metal spatula. The hearts remind us that God loves each one of us!

Cinnamon Toast

(Ingredients on page 10)

Give each child two pieces of bread. Cut a heart out of each piece of bread using a heart-shaped cookie cutter. (The bread scraps can be given to the birds outside. God loves them, too!) Use a plastic knife to spread butter on the heart-shaped bread pieces. Sprinkle cinnamon-sugar mixture on top. Place the bread on cookie sheets and put them in an oven set to broil. The bread will brown quickly, so keep an eye on it. Remind the children that when we see a heart, we can remember that God loves us.

Games:
A Hunt for Hearts

(Supplies on page 10)

Cut large heart shapes from various colors of construction paper. Cut each one in half. Put all the heart pieces in a sack and let each child choose one. When each child has a piece, let the children move about and find their match. The children can hold the two pieces together to make a heart. When all the matches have been made, collect the pieces and put them back in the sack. Play the game

A Happy Heart Craft
Supplies:

red construction paper

scissors

red, pink, or white chenille stems

tape

glue

markers or crayons

heart stickers (optional)

Jiggly Wiggly Hearts Snack
Ingredients:

4 small or 2 large boxes of red gelatin

bowl

measuring cup

2 cups boiling water

spoon

9" x 13" pan

cooking spray

heart-shaped cookie cutter

metal spatula

cinnamon Toast snack Ingredients:

bread

heart-shaped cookie cutter

butter

plastic knives

cinnamon-sugar mixture

cookie sheets

oven (broiler)

A Hunt for Hearts Game Supplies:

construction paper

scissors

sack

music and player (optional)

Heart Ball Game Supplies:

red ball or balloon

marker

again. Play music while the children are moving about. See how many matches have been made when the music stops.

For older preschoolers, use a variety of colors, but cut several hearts of each color. To make this harder for them, cut the hearts in half with different kinds of lines—zigzags, curves, and so forth. The children now have to match the color and the cut. Only one other piece will fit each half.

Heart Ball

Have the children stand in a circle. Have a red ball or a red balloon with a heart drawn on it. The children pass the ball or balloon around the circle. The object is to keep the ball moving and not let it drop to the floor. When the ball comes back to the first person, all the children clap three times as they *say: God loves me!* Then have the children take one step backwards.

The circle just got a little larger, and the space between the children is a little wider. Pass the heart ball around the circle again. The larger the gap between the children, the more likely it is to fall to the floor. If a child drops the ball, anyone can pick it up and give it back to that child. Continue passing the ball around the circle. When the ball has made it all the way around again, the children clap three times as they *say: God loves me!* The children take another step back and continue the game as before. Start the game over when the children are dropping it more than they are catching it.

SONG:

Use the tune "Twinkle, Twinkle Little Star" for these words and add the motions as the song is sung:

I have learned that God loves me.
(Hug self.)

That just fills my heart with glee!
(Tap right hand on heart.)

God loves all the people, too.

That means you and you and you.
(Point to different children.)

I have learned that God loves me.
(Hug self.)

That just fills my heart with glee!
(Tap right hand on heart.)

PRAYER:

Pray: Dear God, Thank you for loving me. I love you, too! Amen.

STEPPING STONES OF FAITH:
GOD CARES ABOUT ALL OF ME

"God cares for you." *(1 Peter 5:7, CEV)*

STEPPING INTO THE BIBLE:
The Birds and the Flowers

(Matthew 6:25-33)

First tell the children the Bible story as is. Then retell the Bible story. Let the boys be the birds and let the girls be the flowers. Every time you **say: birds,** have the boys stand up and flap their wings. When you **say: flowers,** have the girls stand up and raise their arms into the air as if they are blooming flowers. If time allows, read the story again and reverse the roles.

Say: Jesus sat on the ground. Many people followed Jesus wherever he went. They wanted to hear what he had to say. Jesus told the people that God loved them.

Jesus said, "Look at the <u>birds</u> up in the air. They need food to eat every day. The <u>birds</u> do not have a barn to hold extra food. God feeds the <u>birds</u> every day."

Then Jesus said, "And look at the beautiful <u>flowers.</u> They are beautiful because of what God does. The <u>flowers</u> cannot work or make clothes. God makes the <u>flowers</u> beautiful."

colored
construction paper

marker

scissors

glue

wiggle eyes
(optional)

bag of
Magic Nuudles®

small bowl of water

construction paper

"You are more important to God than the birds. You are more special to God than the flowers. If God loves the birds and the flowers, then you can know that God loves you, too."

CRaFTS:
Birdie, Birdie in the Sky

Trace each child's foot on a sheet of construction paper. Let the child cut it out. Trace each child's hand on paper of the same color and cut out two handprints. Glue the handprints to each side of the footprint for wings. Let the child draw eyes or glue wiggle eyes near the top of the footprint. He or she can draw or cut a triangle for the bird's beak. Add two long skinny rectangles for bird legs.

Remind the children that God feeds the birds every day because God cares about them. God cares about us even more than the birds. **Say: If God cares that much about the birds and what they eat, you know that God surely cares about you.**

Flower Power

Use a bag of Magic Nuudles® to make flowers of many beautiful colors. Have each child lightly dampen one end of a green Nuudle® and attach it to the end of another green Nuudle®. Put three or four of these together to make a flower stem. Remember to *lightly* dampen these. If they get too wet, they dissolve.

Use a variety of colors to make the flower part at the top of the stem. Lightly dampen one end of a colored Nuudle® and attach it to the side of the green Nuudle® at the top of the flower stem. Put five or six of these around the top of the stem to make a flower. The tip of the stem shows through for the center of the flower.

It may be better for younger preschoolers if a basic flower shape is drawn for them on construction paper. The children can lightly dampen the Nuudles® and attach them to the paper to fill in the flower.

If Magic Nuudles® are not available in your area, use any flower craft that you are familiar with for craft time with the children. Whatever flower is made, remind the children that God cares about the flowers and makes them beautiful. Tell them that God cares about people even more than flowers. **Say: If God cares that much about the little flowers and "what they wear," you know that God cares about you.**

Snacks:
Crazy Daisies

Make cupcakes ahead of time according to the directions on the cake mix box. Add yellow food coloring to white ready-made frosting until it is bright yellow.

Give each child an unfrosted cupcake. Have him or her spread the frosting onto a cupcake with a plastic knife. Give each child five miniature marshmallows and have him or her flatten them as much as possible. Place one chocolate-coated candy in the center of the cupcake and place the five flattened marshmallows around it to make a daisy.

Remind the children that God cares about the flowers and makes them beautiful. God cares about us even more than the flowers. **Say: The Bible talks about the beautiful flowers that are here today and gone tomorrow. Well, see how fast you can make THESE flowers disappear!**

This Bird's Nest Is the Best!

Melt chocolate and butterscotch chips in a pan over low heat or microwave them in a microwaveable bowl until melted. Pour the melted mixture over chow mien noodles and gently blend them so the noodles are coated. Place waxed paper on a cookie sheet. Put a large spoon of the noodles onto the waxed paper. Shape it to look like a bird's nest. Handle carefully in case it is still warm. Put jelly beans in the nest for eggs. Refrigerate this until it is firm. The children will enjoy eating the jelly beans and the nest.

Say: God cares what the birds have to eat. God cares what the flowers have to wear. God cares about all of your needs, too.

Games:
Egg Hunt

(Supplies on page 14)

Children love to find hidden Easter eggs no matter what time of year it is! Enclose a heart sticker in each egg and hide the eggs in the room. Let the children find them all. Have the children "hatch" their eggs and find the stickers inside. Remind the children that God cares about the birds that hatch from real eggs and what they need. **Say: God cares about all of our needs, too.** Hide the eggs again for another hunt, if time allows.

CRAZY Daisies Snack
Ingredients:

cupcakes

white ready-made frosting

yellow food coloring

plastic knives

miniature marshmallows

chocolate-coated candies

THIS BIRD'S NEST IS THE BEST! Snack
Ingredients:

12-ounce package chocolate chips

12-ounce package butterscotch chips

microwaveable bowl or pan

l large can chow mien noodles

large spoon

cookie sheet

waxed paper

jelly beans

BRINGING IN THE BIRDS GAME Supplies:

hula hoops or masking tape

Bringing in the Birds

Scatter several large round hoops on the floor around the play area. These will be the "nests" for the birds. Choose one child to be the mother or father bird (otherwise known as "It"). The others will be the baby birds. Have the baby birds fly around the room while the mother/father bird tries to catch them and bring them home.

Once a baby bird has been caught, the mother/father bird takes him or her home to the "nest." The little birds must stay in the nest until all the baby birds have been brought safely home. Use more than one hoop so that the children can stand comfortably while waiting in the nest. You may then choose a new "it" and start the game over.

If you have a large group of children, have a mother AND a father bird catching the baby birds. If no hoops are available, use masking tape to make large circle shapes on the floor.

SONG:

Use the tune "Rock-a-Bye Baby" for these words:

God loves the flowers,

Pretty as can be.

God loves the birds

That sit in the tree.

But who does God love

More than these?

God does love you, and God does love me.

PRAYER:

Pray: Dear God, Thank you for caring about all of me—from the top of my head to the tip of my toes! Amen.

STEPPING STONES OF FAITH:
GOD UNDERSTANDS MY FEELINGS

"Our LORD is great and powerful! He understands everything." *(Psalm 147:5, CEV)*

STEPPING INTO THE BIBLE:
The Beatitudes

(Matthew 5:1-12)

Attach seven paper plates to seven paint mixing sticks. Color the plates with different colors and use a black marker to draw a simple face on each one in order to show happy, sad, angry, silly, excited, sleepy, and surprised.

Start by **asking the children: How do you FEEL today? Are you happy today? Are you sad? Is anyone angry?** Show the paper plate faces for happy, sad, and angry as they are mentioned.

Say: Jesus thought that being happy was so important that he spent time talking about it to the people who followed him. Jesus told them how they could be happy.

Jesus told them, "Happy are the people who try to be kind." Jesus was saying, "If you are kind to other people, they will be kind to you."

Ask: How can you be kind? (Let a child respond.)

Say: Jesus said, "Happy are people who want to obey God."

Ask: What can we do to obey and be good? *(follow the rules, listen to our moms and dads)*

Say: Jesus also said, "Happy are people who make peace with other people." Jesus told the people how they could live and be happy. What does it mean to make peace with other people? Give some examples if the children do not respond. *(You can let someone get in front of you in line. You can let your brother have the bigger cookie because you know that you will get a cookie, too. You can let your friend choose what toys to play with when he comes to your house to play.)*

Say: Jesus often had a crowd of people following him. He liked to teach them new things. On that day, Jesus was teaching them how God wanted them to live: God wants us to be kind, God wants us to be good or obey, God wants us to be helpful and loving and make peace with other people. When we do those things, we can be happy people!

But Jesus knew that no one would be happy all the time. So he also told the people: "When you are sad, God will comfort you.

"When you are hurt by someone, God can make you feel better.

"When you try to do the right thing and people make fun of you, God will help you, too." God understands how we feel.

Show the children the face plates. Tell them you want them to make a face to show the same feelings. Encourage the children to repeat the response each time.

Say: **When I am happy,** *(Show the happy face plate.)*

God understands how I feel. (Kids repeat this phrase each time.)

When I am sad, *(Show the sad face.)*

God understands how I feel.

Even when I'm angry, *(Show the angry face.)*

God understands how I feel.

When I feel silly, *(Show the silly face.)*

God understands how I feel.

When I feel excited, *(Show the excited face.)*

God understands how I feel.

Even when I feel sleepy, *(Show the sleepy face.)*

God understands how I feel.

Say: Jesus talked to the people a long time that day. He told them many things about God. The people were surprised at all that Jesus knew. Even if you are "surprised" (Show the surprised face paper plate.) by something, God will understand that, too!

CRAFTS:
My Feelings

Cut a five-inch circle out of the center of a paper plate. Have the child color the rim with crayons. While the child is doing that, cut a one-inch slit at an angle at the top of a short cardboard tube on each side. The child can color the tube, if desired. Write "My Feelings" around the top of the plate rim. Show the child how to insert the plate into the slits in the tube and hold the plate in front of his or her face. Ask the child to show how he or she looks on a happy day. **Ask: How do you look when you feel tired or angry or sad or silly?** Remind the children that God understands how we feel—no matter if we feel sad or angry or silly or scared. **Say: God understands our feelings.**

MY FEELINGS CRAFT Supplies:

9" paper plates

short cardboard tubes

scissors

crayons

marker

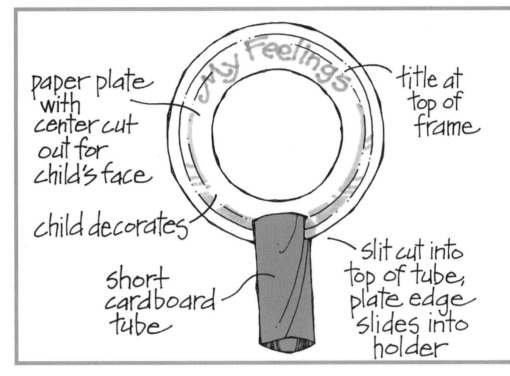

paper plate with center cut out for child's face

child decorates

short cardboard tube

title at top of frame

slit cut into top of tube, plate edge slides into holder

You Can BEE Happy

Give each child a copy of the bee (page 21) and let her or him color it with crayons or markers. Next, give each child a whole paper plate and a half paper plate. Turn the plates so that the bottoms of the plates face outward. Staple the half plate to the whole plate. Let the child glue the bee onto the whole paper plate. The child can insert his or her hand between the plates and fly the bee around the room.

Say: Jesus told the people that God wants us to be happy! When we live like God wants us to live, we can BEE happy!

YOU CAN BEE HAPPY CRAFT Supplies:

bee pattern (page 21)

crayons or markers

9" paper plates

scissors

stapler

glue

front back

"You Can BEE Happy"

glue bee to plate

child inserts hand

2 9-inch paper plates

Bee-nanas Snack Ingredients:

bananas

plastic knives

ready-made chocolate frosting

miniature chocolate-coated candies

spoon

paper plates

pretzel sticks

microwave oven

snacks:
Bee-nanas

If possible, chill the bananas before using them. Cut each banana in half and round the ends so that a half banana looks like a bee body. Warm ready-made chocolate frosting in the microwave in 30-second increments. Do this until the frosting is pourable. Start by putting two dots of frosting at the top where the bee's eyes will go. Attach two miniature chocolate-coated candies to the dots of frosting for eyes. With the bee body on a plate, use a spoon to drizzle the frosting back and forth over the banana to make stripes on the bee. Poke short pretzel sticks in the top to make the bee's antennae. Cut two slices from the leftover portion of the banana. Place the slices on each side of the bee's body for wings.

Say: Jesus told the people that God wants us to be happy! When we live like God wants us to live, we can BEE happy people!

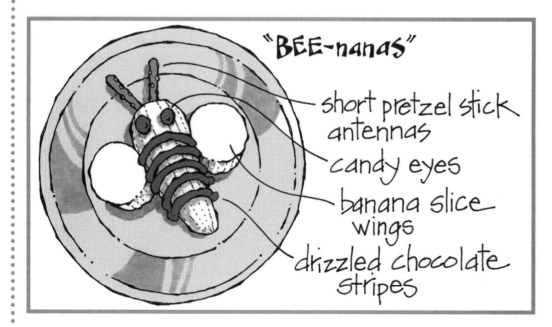

"BEE-nanas"

short pretzel stick antennas

candy eyes

banana slice wings

drizzled chocolate stripes

Making Funny Faces

Give each child a wide-mouth cup with pudding in it. Let the child make a face on the top of the pudding. Because feelings have been discussed, they may want to make a happy face, a sad face, a funny face, or even a mad face. Use miniature candies, miniature marshmallows, raisins, chocolate chips, and licorice to make the facial features. Sprinkle coconut along the top edge for hair, if desired. You can tint the coconut by placing it in a zippered plastic bag and adding a few drops of food coloring. Move the coconut around the bag until it is tinted. Remind the children that no matter how we feel—happy, sad, silly, or mad—God understands how we feel.

Games:
Smile Awhile

Have the children sit in a large circle on the floor. Be "It" first so the children will understand how to play this game. Stand in the center of the circle and smile awhile. Tell the children who are sitting in the circle that they cannot smile. Make funny faces and try to make the children giggle. When you are ready, wipe the smile off your face, call a child by name, and then toss your smile to that child. That child then "catches" the smile and puts it on his or her own face. That child becomes the new "It" and tries to make the other children smile.

No one is "out" of the game if they smile, but you can make it fun by watching for smiles and making the children cover them up! Remind the children that when we live like God wants us to live, we can be happy. We can smile awhile!

Catch the BEE-attitudes

Say: In the Beatitudes, Jesus told the people how God wants us to BE. God wants us to BE kind, God wants us to BE obedient, and God wants us to BE helpful.

Let the children use the bee puppets made earlier for this game. Have the children fly around the room, being careful not to run into the other bees. Choose one child to be the "beekeeper" who is trying to catch the bees. If a bee is caught (a child is tagged), the beekeeper brings the bee to the hive (a hula hoop on the floor or a large circle made with masking tape).

When the hive is fairly full, stop the game. Let the bees that were caught name one way that God wants us to BE, such as "God wants me to BEE kind" or "God wants me to BEE friendly" or "God wants me to BEE obedient." As they give a correct answer, let the bees go free. The children will likely repeat what another child said. That is okay! Choose a new beekeeper and start the game again.

Making Funny Faces Snack
Ingredients:

pudding in wide-mouth cups

miniature candies

miniature marshmallows

raisins

chocolate chips (or white chips)

thin licorice strips

coconut, food coloring, and zippered plastic bag (optional)

spoons

Smile Awhile Game
Supplies:

Catch the BEE-attitudes Game
Supplies:

bee puppets children made earlier

hula hoop or masking tape

SONG:

Use the tune "If You're Happy and You Know It" for these words and add the appropriate motions to the song:

If you're feeling pretty happy, show your smile.

If you're feeling pretty happy, show your smile.

If you're feeling pretty happy, then God will understand.

If you're feeling pretty happy, show your smile.

If you're feeling kinda angry, stomp your feet.

If you're feeling kinda angry, stomp your feet.

If you're feeling kinda angry, then God will understand.

If you're feeling kinda angry, stomp your feet.

Add these other verses if you wish:

feeling kinda sad—cry boo-hoo

feeling kinda sleepy—yawn real big

feeling kinda silly—giggle, giggle

feeling kinda scared—shake, shake, shake

PRAYER:

Pray: Dear God, thank you for helping us know the way we can be happy. We know we can be happy if we are kind to other people, we obey you, and we try to make peace with other people. Amen.

Pattern: You Can BEE Happy

The children will color the bee and glue it to a nine-inch plate. A half plate is stapled to the back of this plate with the bottoms of the plates facing out. This gives the child room to insert his or her hand and "fly" the bee around the room.

STEPPING STONES OF FAITH:
GOD IS ALWAYS WITH ME

"Wherever you go, I will watch over you."
(Genesis 28:15, CEV)

STEPPING INTO THE BIBLE:
David and Goliath
(1 Samuel 17:12-49)

Read the first verse below and have the children echo you. Include the motions as well. This will appear several times in the story. Encourage the children to participate each time it appears.

Start by telling the children that you have a story to tell them about two men named David and Goliath. David was little, and Goliath was big.

David and Goliath—what a pair!

One was here *(Place hand at chest level to show a short man.)*

and one was there!

(Place hand over your head to show a very tall man.)

Goliath stood nine feet high.

He was a giant in everyone's eyes.

He carried a sword and spear in his arms.

He wore his armor so he wouldn't be harmed.

Now David was not very tall,

But he was braver than them all.

He did not like what Goliath had to say.
Goliath was being mean to David's friends that day.

(Have the children repeat this part with you.)
David and Goliath—what a pair!
One was here *(hand at chest level)*
and one was there! *(hand over your head)*

Goliath said, "Come on and fight.
We'll work for you if you win tonight.
But if we win, you have to stay
And work for us every day."
"I'll fight him!" David told the king.
Then he found five rocks to fit in his sling.
"Goliath, I know that God is with me.
God will help me win this, you will see."

(Children say their part.)

David put a rock in his sling.
Over his head, he made it swing.
Round and round the sling did go.
And that rock hit Goliath right above his nose.
Goliath came down, down, down *(say slowly)*
Until his face hit the ground.
"Hooray!" they said. "This was a good day!"
God was with David all the way.

(Children say their part.)

CRAFTS:
The Vest That Wasn't the Best

Before class, cut brown grocery bags to make a vest for each child. Open the bag so that it stands on its flat bottom. Cut a straight line down the front of the bag. When you reach the bottom, continue cutting and make a circle on the flat part of the bag. This circle will be the part that fits around the child's neck (so size it accordingly). On each side of the bag, close to the bottom, cut two circles for armholes. Now turn the bag upside down and there is the vest!

THE Vest THaT wasn't THe Best Craft Supplies:

brown grocery bags

aluminum foil

scissors

glue

white paper

marker

shallow pan or styrofoam meat tray

paint

toy cars or trucks

A GIANT OF A COOKIE SNACK Ingredients:

one box (about 18 ounces) of sugar cookie mix

extra ingredients as listed on the box

bowl and utensils needed

12-inch pizza pan

two-thirds cup miniature chocolate-coated candies

white ready-made frosting

spoon

pizza cutter

Provide sheets of aluminum foil for the children. Let each one cut or tear pieces of foil and glue them to the vest. Help the child put on the armor when he or she is finished. When Goliath was in battle, he wore armor to protect himself. David tried to wear armor, but it was too heavy for him. Remind the children that David knew God was with him. We know that God is always with us, too.

If large brown paper grocery bags are not available, try using the larger size of lunch bags. The children will not be able to wear the vests, of course, but they can still experience making the "armor."

Car Tracks

For each child, title a sheet of white paper "God Is With Me Wherever I Go" or "God Is Always With Me." Pour a shallow layer of paint in a pan. Have the children roll a toy car or truck in the paint. Now have the children "drive" the car all over their papers making car tracks. Roll the car in the paint again and drive some more. Remind the children that we go places in cars and trucks today. **Say: God is always with us wherever we go.**

Snacks: A Giant of a Cookie

Preheat the oven and prepare sugar cookie mix according to the directions on the box. Spread the dough onto an ungreased 12-inch pizza pan. Put miniature chocolate-coated candies on top and gently push them into the dough. Bake the giant cookie for 20 to 24 minutes until it is lightly browned. Microwave white frosting until it is pourable (start with 15-30 seconds). Use a spoon to drizzle this icing back and forth across the cookie. Serve the cookie from the pan once it has cooled.

Show the children the giant-sized cookie before cutting it. Show them a regular-size cookie such as they might have for a snack. Remind the children that Goliath was a giant of a man—much bigger than David. But David called on God to help him, and God was with him all the way! Now use a pizza cutter to cut the cookie and share with everyone in the class.

David's Sling*

Put a pita pocket on a paper plate for each child. Scoop some peanut butter into the pocket for each child and let the child spread it around with a plastic knife or wooden craft stick. Give each child five slices of banana. Have the child count them as you cut them. Let the child put the banana slices inside the pita pocket. Remind the children that David found five rocks to put in his sling, but he only used one. **Say: God was with David when he faced the giant Goliath. God is always with us, too.**

*Be aware of allergies to peanuts and peanut butter.

Games:
Pebble, Pebble, Who Has the Pebble?

Have the children sit in a circle on the floor. Have a helper take one child out of the room. While they are gone, give a pebble to one child and have her or him sit on it. When the other child comes back into the room, **say: Pebble, pebble, who has the pebble?** (Tell the children that a pebble is a small rock.)

Tell the children to clap softly as the child walks around the circle. When "It" gets near the child with the pebble, the children should clap loudly. The child who is "It" then guesses who is sitting on the pebble. Choose a new "It" and play the game again.

When the game is over, show the children the one little pebble. Remind them that David only used one little stone when he was fighting Goliath. **Say: He was a little guy with a big job, but God helped David. God was with David wherever he went. God will always be with us, too.**

Oh, the Places I Can Go

Have the children sit on the floor. Choose one child to come to the front and name a place that he or she likes to go. It could be the store, Grandma's house, or even school. **Say: [Child's name] likes to go to [repeat what the child said].** Have the children all *respond: God is with me wherever I go.* As they say this, have them clap on each word.

Choose another child to come to the front and do the same thing. Continue until each child has had a turn. Each time a child names a place to go, have the children *respond: God is with me wherever I go.* Change the clapping to stomping or slapping their legs or even patting their tummies.

David's Sling Snack
Ingredients:

paper plates

pita pockets

peanut butter

bananas

plastic knives or wooden craft sticks

Pebble, Pebble, Who Has the Pebble? Game
Supplies:

one pebble

Oh, the Places I Can Go Game
Supplies:

SONG:

Use the tune for "Where Is Thumbkin?" with these words:

God is with me.

God is with me,

Where I go,

Where I go.

God is always with me.

God is always with me,

Where I go,

Where I go.

Have all the children sing all the words or divide them into two groups. One group sings the first line and the second group echoes them.

PRAYER:

Pray: Dear God,

If I go to school, you are with me.

If I go outside to play, you are with me.

If I go to my Grandma's house, you are with me there, too.

You are ALWAYS with me! Thank you!

Amen.

STEPPING STONES OF FAITH:
GOD WILL HELP ME WHEN I AM AFRAID

"The Lord is on my side, and I am not afraid of what others can do to me." *(Psalm 118:6, CEV)*

STEPPING INTO THE BIBLE:
Daniel in the Lions' Den
(Daniel 6:1-27)

Make two puppets of any kind: paper bags, socks, wooden spoons, or so forth. Make one with a crown on his head to be the king. The other puppet will be Daniel. Show the king puppet when talking about the king. Show the Daniel puppet when talking about Daniel.

Show the Daniel puppet.

Say: Daniel was a hard worker. He worked for the king. The king liked Daniel. Daniel loved God, and he prayed to God every day.

Show the king puppet.

One day the king made a new rule. The rule said that no one who lived in the king's land should pray to anyone but the king. If anyone disobeyed, then he would be thrown into a den of hungry lions!

Show the Daniel puppet.

Daniel did not want to pray to the king. He wanted to pray to God. Daniel prayed three times every day. Some people saw Daniel through the window of his house. Daniel was praying to God. They told the king what Daniel was doing.

Show the king puppet.

The king was sad. The king liked Daniel. He did not want to put Daniel in the den of hungry lions, but he had to follow the new rule. The king told his helpers to put Daniel in the lions' den!

Would you be afraid if you were in a den of hungry lions?

Show the king puppet.

The king could not sleep that night. He was worried about Daniel. He was afraid the hungry lions would eat Daniel! The next morning, the king went to check on Daniel. Would he be alive? The king said, "Daniel, did God save you from the lions?"

Show the Daniel puppet.

Was Daniel okay? Would he answer the king? Yes, Daniel was okay. He said, "Yes, I am here. God sent an angel to take care of me. The angel shut the mouths of the hungry lions."

Show the king puppet.

The king was happy! He made a new rule. The rule said everyone should pray to God just like Daniel did. God had taken care of Daniel.

Teach the children the following song to the tune of "Did You Ever See a Lassie?" Emphasize Daniel's name every time you sing it, and have the children clap or stomp when they hear Daniel's name.

Show the Daniel puppet.

Dare to be like <u>Daniel</u>,

Like <u>Daniel</u>, like <u>Daniel</u>.

Dare to be like <u>Daniel</u>.

Remember to pray.

Like <u>Daniel</u>, like <u>Daniel</u>, like <u>Daniel</u>, like <u>Daniel</u>,

Dare to be like <u>Daniel</u>.

Remember to pray.

CRafts:
PAWS to Pray

Using the paw print patterns (page 32), cut two paw prints for each child from construction paper. Have the child put his or her finger on a black stamp pad and make a little fingerprint on each of the lion's toes. Now put the child's thumb

PAWS to PRay CRaft Supplies:

paw print patterns
(page 32)

orange or yellow
construction paper

scissors

black stamp pad

hand-cleaning
supplies

yarn

glue or tape

marker

on the stamp pad. Make a thumbprint for the large pad in the middle of the lion's paw. Do this on both paws. Have the child clean the ink off her or his hand. Cut yarn into 9-inch lengths. Attach a paw print to each end of the yarn. On the back of one paw print, write "PAWS …" On the back of the other paw print, write "to pray!" The joined paw prints can be used as a bookmark.

Talk to the children about things that make them afraid. Remind them that God will help them when they are afraid—they can "Paws to Pray" and God will help them.

CD Lion

Obtain a discarded CD or CD-ROM for each child. This is a good way to recycle CD-ROMs that arrive in the mail. Cut yellow circles the same size as a CD. Let each child draw a lion's face on a circle and glue this circle on top of a CD. Cut a 14" length of fishing line. Knot the two ends together to make a loop. Securely tape the knotted end of the fishing line to the back of the CD at the top of the lion's head. Now cut a large cloud shape from orange paper. This should be larger than the CD. When glued to the back of the CD, it will be the lion's mane. This will also cover the spot where the fishing line was attached. On the back of the lion's mane, write "Don't be scared—say a prayer!" Read this to the children. Remind them that when they are afraid, they can pray to God just like Daniel did.

Snacks:
Would You Ever Eat a Lion?

Use animal cookies for a snack. Give each child several different animals. Before eating them, play a game. **Say: Lion, lion, who has a lion?** Any child who has a lion cookie should hold it in the air. Let each child eat one animal cookie. Next, **say: Bear, bear, who has a bear?** The children who have bear cookies hold them in the air, and then they all eat one more cookie. Do this several times with other animals. Children always love seeing what animals they have to eat!

Remind the children that God helped Daniel when he was with the scary lions. **Say: God will help us when we are afraid, too.**

Daniel's Den-ner

Clean and cut vegetables for the children to eat. Try carrot sticks, cucumbers, and broccoli. Provide dip for the children to use with their vegetables. Tell the children that Daniel ate only vegetables (Daniel 1:1-16) when he worked for the king. When that king had Daniel put in with the hungry lions, Daniel knew that God would help him. He did not need to be afraid.

CD Lion Craft Supplies:

discarded CDs or CD-ROMs

yellow and orange construction paper

scissors

markers

glue

fishing line

wide sturdy tape

Would You Ever Eat a Lion? Snack Ingredients:

animal cookies

Daniel's Den-ner Snack Ingredients:

vegetables

knife

dip

spoon

plates

29

posterboard

marker

scissors

masking tape

box

beanbags

GAMES:
Lion Toss

Cut a large lion face from posterboard. Cut a round hole for the mouth. Attach the lion to a large open box. Make a line on the floor with masking tape to show the children where to stand as they try to toss beanbags into the lion's mouth. If they make it in, they get to reach inside the lion's mouth and pull it out! **Ask: Are you afraid now?**

Say: Of course, this is a fun game; but if we really do feel afraid at some time, God will really help us.

Daniel, Daniel, in the Lion's Den

Have the children form a circle and hold hands. Choose one child to be Daniel and stand in the center of the circle. Choose another child to be the lion and stand outside the circle. The lion will try to enter the circle and get to Daniel, but the children holding hands will try to keep the lion out.

The children are to hold their hands together as they *chant:*

Daniel, Daniel, in the lion's den.

The lion's on the OUTSIDE but he (she) wants IN!

The lion walks around the outside of the circle and tries to get in. The children keep their hands together in the air until they see the lion coming near. If the lion tries to sneak inside the circle between two children, they can put their arms down quickly. The children have to be alert to keep the lion away from Daniel.

Give the lion three chances to get through any of the gates. If the lion gets in, he or she can be the new Daniel. If he or she does not get in, choose a new Daniel and a new lion. If there is a large group of children, have two lions pacing outside the circle.

Remind the children that being in a den of lions was a scary thing that happened to Daniel. God helped Daniel. **Say: If you are ever afraid, God will help you, too.**

SONG:

Use the tune "Did You Ever See a Lassie?" for the following words. Emphasize Daniel's name every time it is sung. Have the children clap or stomp every time they hear his name.

Dare to be like <u>Daniel,</u>

Like <u>Daniel,</u> like <u>Daniel.</u>

Dare to be like <u>Daniel.</u>

Remember to pray.

Like <u>Daniel,</u> like <u>Daniel,</u> like <u>Daniel,</u> like <u>Daniel,</u>

Dare to be like <u>Daniel.</u>

Remember to pray.

PRAYER:

Pray: Dear God, when Daniel was afraid, you helped him be brave and strong. When I am afraid, I know you will help me, too. Amen.

Pattern: PAWS to Pray

Give each child two paw prints. Each child will put a finger onto a stamp pad and make a print for each toe on the paw print. Then he or she will attach one paw print to each end of a 9-inch length of yarn, and it can be inserted in a book or Bible as a bookmark. Write on the back of one "PAWS …" and on the back of the other one "to pray!"

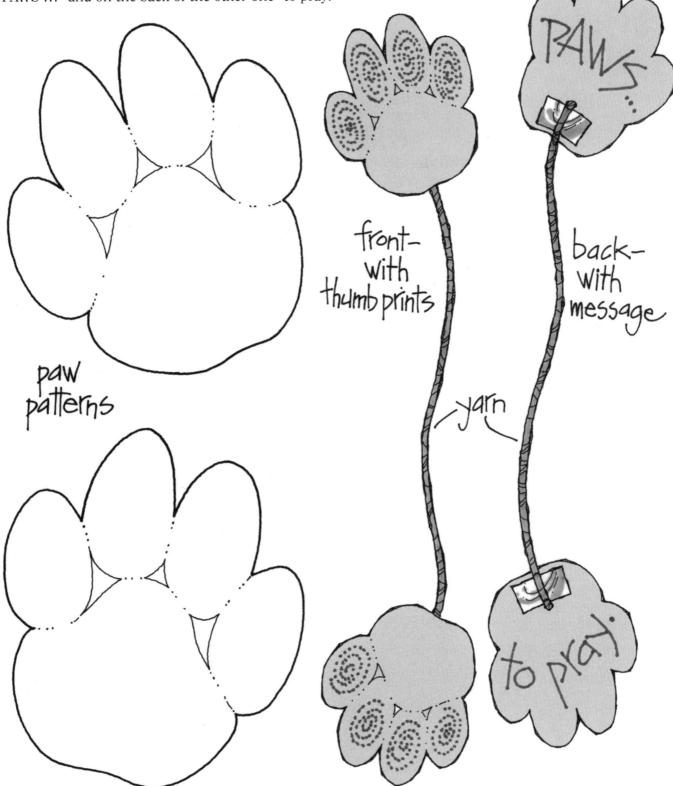

paw patterns

front—with thumb prints

back—with message

PAWS

yarn

to pray

STEPPING STONES OF FAITH:
GOD WILL LISTEN WHEN I PRAY

"The Lord watches over everyone who obeys him, and he listens to their prayers." *(1 Peter 3:12, CEV)*

STEPPING INTO THE BIBLE:
Jonah and the Big Fish
(Jonah 1:1–3:3)

Make the movements during the story, and invite the children to join along. Briefly retell the story by using the motions again.

Say: Sailing. Sailing.

(Pretend to rock back and forth as in a boat.)

God spoke to Jonah one day. God told Jonah to go to a city called Nineveh and tell the people there about God. Jonah heard that Nineveh was a bad place to go. He was afraid to go. Jonah did not listen to God. He got on a boat going in the other direction!

Raining. Raining.

(Pretend it is raining. Start with hands high in front and move them downward. Wiggle fingers as your hands move down.)

33

While Jonah was on that boat, it began to rain. It did not just rain—it stormed! Jonah knew that he could not hide from God. He told the men on the boat to throw him overboard, and the storms would stop. They did not want to throw him overboard. They did not want Jonah to drown. They tried to row the boat to shore, but the storms were too strong. So the men did as Jonah said.

Swimming. Swimming.

(Pretend to swim by moving arms as if swimming.)

When Jonah was thrown into the sea, the storms stopped just like Jonah had said they would. Along came a big, big fish and swallowed Jonah whole. He stayed in the belly of this big fish for three days and three nights. From inside the belly of the fish, Jonah prayed.

Praying. Praying.

(Pretend to pray by putting hands together under chin.)

God heard Jonah. The big fish spit Jonah out on dry land. God listened to Jonah when he prayed. Then God told Jonah again to go to Nineveh and tell the people there about God.

Sailing. Sailing.

(Pretend to rock back and forth as in a boat.)

This time Jonah listened to God. Jonah went to Nineveh and talked to the people about God.

CRAFTS:
What a Whale!

Trace the whale pattern (page 37) on construction paper for each child and help her or him to cut it out. Glue the whale to one side of a cube-shaped tissue box. Insert a tissue in the top of the box where the tissues normally pull out. The whale is blowing his spout! You can even use a new box of tissues for each child. Every time the child needs to "blow," she or he will be reminded of Jonah's days in the belly of the big fish.

WHat a WHale! Craft Supplies:

whale pattern (page 37)

pencil

blue or gray construction paper

scissors

glue

cube tissue boxes

tissues

If it is not possible to have one tissue box per child, use the same whale pattern and have the child cut it out. Then simply glue a tissue to the back of the whale to make his spout.

tissue "spout"

square tissue box behind whale, or just tape tissue to top of whale

Any Time Night or Day

Cut construction paper so that each child has a piece that is 15" long and 6" wide. Fold the paper in half so that it is 7 1/2" x 6" and keep the fold at the top. Trace the child's right hand on one half of the paper with the fingers almost touching the fold at the top. Do the same with the left hand on the other half of the paper. Now fold under one inch at each end of the paper. When this is folded and standing up, there are praying hands!

Under the handprint on one side, write "Any time night or day …" Under the handprint on the other side, write "God will listen when I pray." Lay the paper flat, and let each child decorate the handprints by providing collage-type supplies. When every child has completed her or his artwork, fold the paper again along the three creases made earlier and stand it up like a triangle. Tape the loose ends together inside the triangle.

Say: Jonah prayed to God, and God listened when he prayed. We can pray to God, too. Any time night or day, God will listen when WE pray!

ANY TIME NIGHT OR DAY CRAFT

Supplies:

12" x 18" colored construction paper

scissors or paper cutter

marker

glitter, stickers, crayons, markers, confetti pieces, and so forth

glue

tape

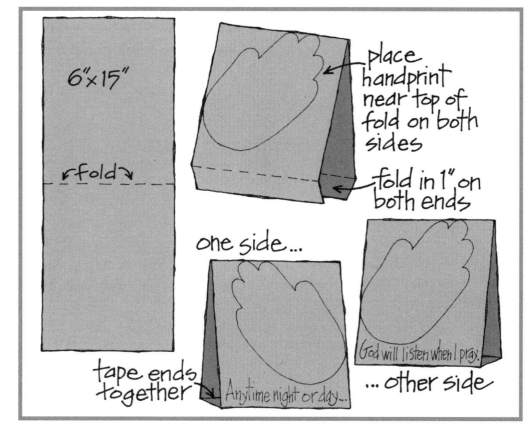

6"x15"

←fold→

place handprint near top of fold on both sides

fold in 1" on both ends

one side...

God will listen when I pray.

...other side

tape ends together

Anytime night or day...

Snacks:
Gingerbread Jonah

Give each child a gingerbread man-shaped cookie on a paper plate. Put frosting in a frosting tube and use it as "glue" for attaching candies to decorate the cookie as a pretend Jonah. **Say: Jonah prayed to God. God listened to Jonah.**

GINGERBREAD JONAH SNACK

Ingredients:

gingerbread man-shaped cookies

paper plates

frosting

frosting tube

candies to decorate cookie

Fish Frenzy

Give each child a blue plate. Add goldfish or whale-shaped crackers to the "sea" for a snack.

GaMes:

How "Whale" Did You Listen?

Say: Jonah stayed in the belly of the big fish for three days and nights. Make three body movements that the children have to imitate. Movements might include clapping, stomping, patting a leg, or other such movements that make sounds. Have the children "listen" and then repeat the three sounds you made. Remind the children that they have to listen to play the game. **Say: God listened to Jonah when he prayed. God will listen when we pray, too.**

"Water" You Going to Paint?

Take the children outside to a concrete or blacktop area where they are safe. Dip a paintbrush in a water bucket and try to paint a picture before it disappears. Let the children try. **Say: Jonah was thrown overboard from the boat into the water. God provided a big fish to come along and swallow Jonah whole.**

SONG:

Use the tune for "Hot Cross Buns" and sing these words:

> **Any time,**
>
> **Night or day,**
>
> **God will listen,**
>
> **God will listen**
>
> **When I pray.**

PRaYeR:

Pray: Dear God,

Any time night or day,

You will listen when I pray.

I am praying right now, and I know you are listening.

Amen.

Pattern: What a Whale!

This large whale can be traced onto construction paper for the children to cut. It will then be glued onto the front of a cube-shaped tissue box. The spout of the whale will be the tissue coming out of the top of the box, so the whale needs to be as tall as the box.

STEPPING STONES OF FAITH:
GOD LIKES TO BE PRAISED

"The LORD is great and deserves our greatest praise!" *(Psalm 96:4, CEV)*

STEPPING INTO THE BIBLE:
David Praises God

(2 Samuel 22:1-4; Psalm 148; Psalm 150)

Say: David was the king. David loved God. He wrote songs to praise God. He wrote songs to show other people that he loved God.

"Everyone should praise God!" David said. The sun and moon should praise God. The animals should praise God. The mountains and hills should praise God. All the children should praise God. All the grown-ups should praise God."

How do we praise God? We can sing. We can play music. We can talk to God in prayer. We can go to church and praise God there, too.

"Everyone should praise God!" David said.

Play a CD with a praise song that the children likely know. Encourage them to sing along, or use the song at the end of this lesson that says "It's good to praise the Lord." As the song is sung, add motions. Every time "praise the Lord" is sung, clap (or stomp, pat your legs, move your head back and forth) three times on those three words. Change the motions each time the verse is sung.

38

CRAFTS:
Instruments of Praise

This section contains four separate ideas for instruments the children can make. Offer a variety of supplies and let each child choose which instrument he or she wishes to make. These will make a nice preschool band when they are used later.

Cymbals
aluminum pie pan
yarn loop to slide hand into

Shakers
8oz. water bottle
decorated label
aquarium rocks

Tambourines
a sturdy plate, children color it
jingle bells

Streamers
fold
paper plate, folded in half
decorated by children
streamers

Cymbals

Let the child decorate the bottom sides of two aluminum pie pans with permanent markers. Poke two holes in the center of each pie pan about two inches apart so that it looks like a giant silver button. Hammer over the holes on the inside and outside of the pie pan so that any sharp edges will be hammered down. Thread yarn through the holes, but do not tie it yet. Have the child place one hand under the yarn. Tie the yarn on the inside of the pie pan so that it fits loosely over the child's hand. This will allow the child to slip his or her hands in and out easily. Do this with each pie pan.

CYMBALS

aluminum pie pans

permanent markers

something to punch holes in pie pans

hammer

6″ pieces of heavy yarn

SHAKERS

miniature (8-ounce) water bottles

colored aquarium rocks

hot-glue gun

construction paper

scissors

crayons or markers

glue

TAMBOURINES

small sturdy paper plates

hole punch

crayons

ribbon or chenille stems

large jingle bells

STREAMERS

6-inch or 9-inch paper plates

crayons or markers

stickers

crepe paper streamers

tape

stapler

Shakers

Give the child a miniature (8-ounce) water bottle. Pour colored aquarium rocks into the bottle. Use a hot-glue gun and attach the lid to the top of the water bottle. While the glue is hardening, cut a strip of construction paper the same size as the label around the water bottle. Let the child decorate it with crayons or markers. You can even write on it "God likes to be praised." Glue the new label to the bottle. Now shake, shake, shake!

Tambourines

Punch five holes in the rim around a paper plate. Have the child color both sides of the paper plate as desired. Thread ribbon or a short piece of a chenille stem through the loop at the top of a jingle bell and through a hole on the plate. Fasten securely. Attach five bells this way. If the chenille stems are used to attach the bells, be sure that the ends are bent inward so they will not poke the child's hand.

Streamers

This instrument does not make a sound, but it can still be used as a way of praising God. Give the child a 6" or a 9" paper plate to color with crayons or markers. Give him or her stickers to add for decorations. Fold the plate in half. Attach colorful crepe paper streamers about 8" or 10" long to the rounded edge. Tape the streamers in place. Staple the rounded edges of the plate together. The children can hold the plates along the folded edge and wave them in the air as they move to the praise music.

Remind the children that we can praise God in many ways. **Say: We can sing. We can play music. We can talk to God in prayer. We can go to church and praise God there, too. We can praise God with cymbals, shakers, tambourines, and even pretty streamers. God likes to hear our praise!**

Snacks:
Praise Pretzels

Pour chocolate (or other flavor) chips into a microwaveable bowl. Cover it with plastic wrap and turn one corner back to vent. Microwave the chips for about one minute and stir. Handle the bowl carefully because it will be hot. Microwave for 30 seconds more and check the chips. Continue this until the chips are completely melted. Let the child dip one half of a pretzel rod into the melted chips. Pour some sprinkles onto a small plate and immediately have the child roll the pretzel rod in the sprinkles. (Sprinkles can add festivity to any food project!) Put the pretzel on a cooling rack while the chocolate hardens. Put some waxed paper under the cooling rack to catch any drippings.

Tell the children that these are "Praise Pretzels." **Say: They remind us that God loves to hear our praise.**

Praise Pretzels Snack

Ingredients:

pretzel rods

bag of flavored chips (chocolate, butterscotch, etc.)

microwaveable bowl

plastic wrap

spoon

sprinkles

small plate

cooling racks

waxed paper

Praise Parfait

Mix instant vanilla pudding according to the directions on the box. Let each child put a layer of pudding in a clear cup. Add a layer of fruit pieces like bananas, strawberries, blueberries, or cantaloupe. Add another layer of pudding, another layer of fruit, and a top layer of pudding. Top it off with festive sprinkles! **Say: Praise is like a celebration. It makes God happy to hear our praise.**

GAMES:
A Praise Parade

As they listen to music, have the children march around the room using the instruments they made earlier. **Say: God likes to hear our praise, and God likes to see this Praise Parade of Preschoolers!**

Praise Relay

Make a starting line on the floor with masking tape. Place chairs at the end of the relay. In each chair, put a bell or other easy-to-play instrument. Group the children in one line or two for this relay. Use two lines if a helper is available to guide the other line. Have the children stand behind the starting line, run to the chair, ring the bell, put it back in the chair, and run back to the starting line. Then guide the child to the back of the line or to a sitting place, and let the next child in line have a turn. Relays are new to preschoolers. Start this slow and build speed as they understand the relay. This does not even have to be a race. The purpose of the relay is for each child to have a chance to "praise the Lord."

SONG:

Use the tune "Shoo Fly" for these words:

> **It's good to praise the Lord.**
>
> **It's good to praise the Lord.**
>
> **It's good to praise the Lord.**
>
> **Everybody praise the Lord!**

Each time the three words "praise the Lord" are sung, add three motions. Clap three times, stomp three times, slap your legs three times, or even blink your eyes three times. **Say: God likes to hear our praise!**

PRAYER:

Pray: Dear God, you are a wonderful God, and you deserve our greatest praise! We've praised you today, and we hope that you have enjoyed it. Amen.

**PRAISE PARFAIT SNACK
Ingredients:**

instant vanilla pudding mix

milk

bowl

mixer or whisk

spoons

fruit pieces

sprinkles

clear cups

**A PRAISE PARADE GAME
Supplies:**

instruments made earlier

recorded music and player

**PRAISE RELAY GAME
Supplies:**

bells or other easy-to-use instruments

masking tape

chairs

STEPPING STONES OF FAITH: GOD WANTS ME TO HELP OTHER PEOPLE

"We should help people whenever we can."
(Galatians 6:10, CEV)

STEPPING INTO THE BIBLE: A Boy Helps Jesus

(John 6:1-14)

Before the children arrive put a pad of paper and a pen inside a picnic basket.

Ask the children if any of them have ever been on a picnic, and let them respond. Tell the children that you are going on a picnic, and it is your job to pack the picnic basket; but you do not know what you need. Open the basket and show the children that all that is inside is a pad of paper and a pen. Ask them for their help with ideas! Write down the children's ideas on paper. Thank them for being such good helpers with all their wonderful ideas!

Say: **I'm excited about going on this picnic! I will have good things to put in my picnic basket once I go to the store. This reminds me of a little boy who went to see Jesus one day. His Mom packed him a lunch. She gave him two fish to eat and five pieces of bread.**

Jesus was busy. Many people had come to see him. Many people had come to hear Jesus teach. It had been a long day, and Jesus knew the people were getting tired and hungry. Jesus asked his helpers to give the people something to eat.

Philip was one of Jesus' helpers. Philip said, "Oh, Jesus, we can't feed all these people! We do not have enough money to buy that much food! There are five thousand people here!" Andrew was another one of Jesus' helpers. He told Jesus, "Here's a little boy who has a lunch with him. He only has two fish and five loaves of bread. That won't be enough to feed this many people. Right, Jesus?" But Jesus said, "Bring that food to me."

Jesus pulled out the bread, and he thanked God for it. Then he told his helpers to give some bread to everyone there. He did the same with the fish. He thanked God for the food. There was enough food for everyone! They ate until their tummies were full!

After all the people had eaten, Jesus told his helpers to pick up the leftover food. They filled twelve baskets with food! Jesus had fed more than five thousand people with just two pieces of fish and five small loaves of bread—all because one little boy shared his lunch! What a good helper he was!

That little boy reminds me of you boys and girls. He was a good helper to Jesus, and you are good helpers to me. Show the children the picnic basket again. **Say: Our Bible tells us, "We should help people whenever we can"** (Galatians 6:10, CEV). **What are some other ways that we can help people?** Let the children name a few ways they can be helpers. Have a few suggestions ready to offer as well.

CRAFTS:
How Can I Help?

Preschoolers can be helpers, too. The children will begin making this fish, but they will finish it by being good helpers at home. Start by giving each child a clear plastic cup. Turn it on its side. The open end will be the fish's mouth. Have fish fins and tails (from the patterns on page 47) cut from construction paper to match the colors of cotton balls available. Help each child attach a tail to the closed end of the cup by taping the tab to the cup. Do the same with the fins, taping one to each side of the cup. Now have the child glue a large wiggle eye on each side of the cup near the fish's mouth.

HOW CAN I HELP? CRAFT Supplies:

clear plastic 12- or 16-ounce cups

fish tail and fin patterns (page 47)

construction paper

tape

large wiggle eyes

glue

colored cotton balls

zippered plastic bags

kids toss cotton balls

into cup each time they help at home

tape fin tabs to 12 or 16 ounce cups as shown

Let each child count about ten colored cotton balls to put in a zippered bag to carry home. Explain to the children that when they are good helpers at home, they can add a cotton ball inside the fish. The more they help, the more colorful the fish will become. You may wish to include a note to the parents so they understand the project and can encourage their child to be a good helper at home.

Say: Jesus was glad that the little boy was a helper. He shared his lunch, and Jesus was able to feed five thousand people with that little bit of food. Jesus wants us to be good helpers, too.

Helping Hands Banner

For each child turn a piece of large construction paper so that it is 12 inches wide and 18 inches long. To make a banner, cut a large upside down "V" out of the bottom edge. Now fold down one and one-half inches at the top of the paper. Near the fold, title the paper "My Helping Hands." Photocopy the words to the song "A Helper I Will Be" (page 48) and have the child glue the lyrics near the bottom of the paper.

Now have the child make handprints all over the banner. Fold several paper towels so that they fit in the bottom of a shallow pan. Pour a layer of paint over the paper towels. This works like a stamp pad so the child does not get too much paint on her or his hand at one time. Having several colors of paint makes this banner quite colorful! Just wipe the child's hand clean with a baby wipe in between colors.

As the handprints dry, write the child's name and the date on the banner. Then fold the flap at the top over the straight bar on a plastic hanger. Use wide tape to hold it down. The child can now hang the "Helping Hands" banner over a door knob at home as a reminder that God wants us to help other people.

HELPING HANDS BANNER CRAFT Supplies:

12" x 18" construction paper

scissors

black marker

song lyrics (page 48)

glue

shallow pans

paper towels

paints

baby wipes

plastic hangers

wide tape

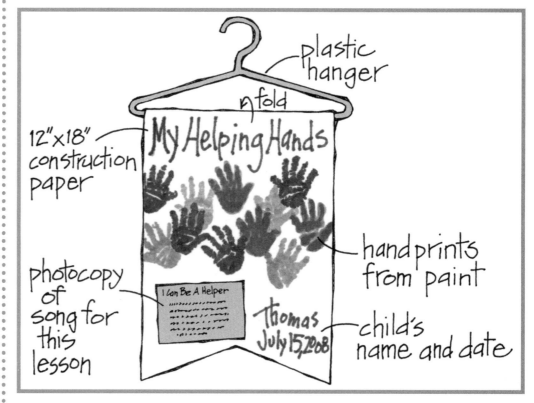

Snacks:
The Little Boy's Lunch

Let the children count out two goldfish crackers and five oyster crackers to start their snacks. Remind them of the little boy who helped Jesus by sharing his lunch. He had two fish and five loaves of bread in his lunch. The children can have more crackers than this to snack on—simply scoop more fish and "bread" onto their plates.

Another option is to have "helpers" who scoop the fish and bread onto the plates. As time is spent with the children today, find as many ways as possible to let them be helpers. Commend them for doing such good jobs. Remind the children that God wants us to help people whenever we can.

I Had a Hand in This Snack!

Give each child a cup that has one of the ingredients for this snack mix. Several children will have the same ingredient. Let each child carry her or his cup to a large bowl and pour in the ingredient. Once all of the children have added their ingredients, use your hands (with plastic gloves on) to mix all the ingredients together. Give each child a coffee filter for a plate. Scoop some of the snack mix out for each child. Comment on how nice it was that everyone helped make the snack today. **Say: Because of all our helpers, we have a variety of things to eat.** Remind the children of the little boy who helped Jesus by sharing his lunch.

Games:
Go Fishing

Gather the children in a large circle on the floor. Choose one child to be the "fisherman." He or she walks around the outside of the circle and taps two children on the head. Those two children and the "fisherman" run around the circle and try to get into the empty spots in the circle. The one left standing is the new "fisherman."

Once a child is tapped on his or her head, he or she will be eager to run. Remind the children that the fisherman has to count two fish before anyone runs. **Say: The little boy had two fish in his lunch that he shared with Jesus. What a good helper he was! God wants us to be good helpers, too.**

THE LITTLE BOY'S LUNCH SNACK

Ingredients:

goldfish-shaped crackers

oyster crackers

I HAD A HAND IN THIS SNACK!

Ingredients:

variety of finger foods (cereal pieces, raisins, chocolate chips, pretzels, and so forth)

small paper cups

large bowl

one pair of plastic gloves

coffee filters

GO FISHING GAME

Supplies:

two or three
bed pillows

masking tape

treats

Pillow Pals

Mark a start and finish line on the floor with masking tape. Call out two children from the group to be "pillow pals." Those two children have to stand facing each other and put a pillow between their tummies. They cannot hold the pillow; but they can hug each other, if they need to, as they walk to the finish line. Once they "help" each other to the finish line without dropping the pillow, they can be given a treat to enjoy. Depending on the age of the group and the number of helpers, it might be fun to have two or three pairs going at the same time. If the pillow falls, the children can pick it up, put it back between their tummies, and continue on. Play until each child has had a turn and has gotten a treat.

SONG:

Use the tune "The Farmer in the Dell" for this song:

> **A helper I will be.**
>
> **A helper I will be.**
>
> **God can use a helper**
>
> **Just like you or me.**

PRAYER:

Pray: Dear God, we're glad that we are big enough to be your helpers. Please help us see things we can do to help others. Amen.

The children will use a 12- or 16-ounce clear cup and turn it into a fish. Turn the cup on its side. The open end is the mouth of the fish. The tail will go on the cup's bottom and the fins will go on each side as the cup is lying down.

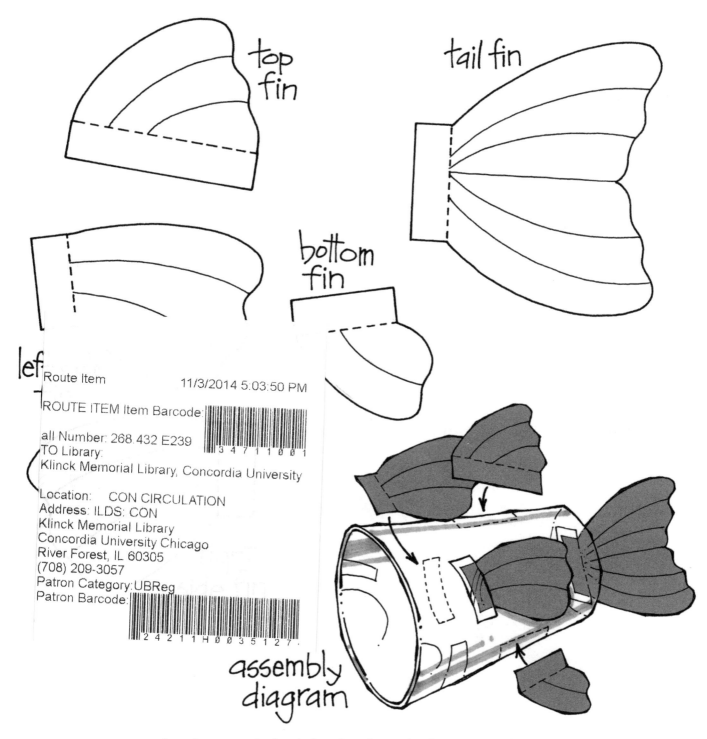

top fin

tail fin

bottom fin

left

assembly diagram

Pattern: Helping Hands Banner

A Helper I Will Be

(to the tune of "Farmer in the Dell")

A helper I will be.
A helper I will be.
God can use a helper
Just like you or me.

A Helper I Will Be

(to the tune of "Farmer in the Dell")

A helper I will be.
A helper I will be.
God can use a helper
Just like you or me.

STEPPING STONES OF FAITH:
GOD KEEPS PROMISES

"I will always keep the promise I have made to you ... because I am your God." *(Genesis 17:7, CEV)*

STEPPING INTO THE BIBLE:
Baby Jesus Is Born
(Matthew 1:18–2:11)

This activity requires a baby doll wrapped in a blanket, one of the angels made in today's lesson, a star, and a happy face drawn on paper. Pass each item around as it is talked about. Once the item has returned, continue telling the story.

Show the children the baby doll wrapped in a blanket.

Say: Isn't my baby doll lovely? When we come to church, we hear a lot about Jesus. Did you know that Jesus was born as a baby just like you and me?

Show the children the angel.

Say: His mother's name was Mary. An angel came to Mary and told her that she was going to have a baby! Then the angel went to Joseph and told him that Mary was going to have a baby. The angel also told Joseph, "When the baby is born, name him Jesus."

Show the children the star.

Say: One day there was a bright star in the sky. Some wise men who watched the stars saw it, and they knew it was special. They followed the star. As they walked, the star moved in

49

front of them. It stopped right over the house where Jesus was. The men went in the house and saw little Jesus there with his mother. They bowed down in front of Jesus and gave him the gifts they had brought for him.

Show the children the happy face.

Say: A long time ago before Jesus was even born, God made a promise. Do you know what a promise is? A promise means saying you will do something and then doing it. It is good to keep promises. God promised the people a long time ago that Jesus would be born. Jesus would be a special helper for them. When the wise men saw the star and found little Jesus, they knew that God's promise had come true! God did what God promised. That made the people happy!

Crafts:
Angel Art

Let the children make an angel craft as a reminder of the story. Give each child a round, sturdy, divided paper plate. Turn it over and place the largest section at the top. This section will be the face of the angel. Use blue star stickers for the two eyes and draw a smile with a marker or crayon. Then have the child use a red stamp pad to make a thumb print nose and cheeks on the angel's face. Attach yarn (in any color), gift bag crinkle paper, or even gold tree tinsel to make hair for the angel. Run a wide line of glue around the top arch of the plate and have the child place the hair there. Bend a gold chenille stem into the shape of a halo and staple it to the other side of the plate so that it stands up behind the angel's head. In the smaller sections of the plate, the children can spread a thin layer of glue and sprinkle gold glitter on top. Pick up the plate and shake off any loose glitter that remains. Remind the children that the angel told Mary and Joseph

ANGEL ART CRAFT Supplies:

sturdy divided paper plates

blue star stickers

markers or crayons

red stamp pad

yarn, gift bag crinkle paper, or gold tinsel

glue

gold chenille stems

stapler

gold glitter

Angel Art — chenille stem / Christmas tinsel / gold glitter / eyes=star stickers / nose and cheeks= stamp pad thumbprints

that they were going to have a baby. **Say: This was great news! God had promised this long ago, and God keeps promises.**

Little Baby in the Manger

Each child will need a plastic cup from individual servings of Pringles® potato chips. Have him or her place some yellow crinkle gift bag paper in the plastic cup. Let the child draw a face on one end of a wooden ice cream spoon. Cut a piece of felt so that it is approximately four inches square. Place it on the table in front of the child so that it looks like a diamond. Place the head of the wooden spoon at the top of the diamond. Fold any excess felt at the bottom of the spoon upward and glue it in place on the spoon. Now wrap the right and left sides around the "baby" and place him in the plastic-cup manger. **Say: God promised long ago that Jesus would be born. God keeps promises.**

Snacks:
A Star of a Sandwich

Make five sandwiches for every four children. Use a sandwich spread or lunch meat of some kind. Any kind of sandwich will do. Cut the sandwiches diagonally so that there are four triangles from each sandwich. Each child will need five triangles—that is why five sandwiches are made for every four children. Place one triangle sandwich at the top of a paper plate with its point facing outward. Now place a triangle on the left side and one on the right side with those points also pointing outward. The final two triangles will be at the bottom with the points facing downward. All the straight edges are on the inside. Place grapes

A Star of a Sandwich

1 sandwich, cut into 4 triangles

each child needs 5 triangles

5 sandwich triangles make a star

fruit in center of star

plastic cups from individual servings of Pringles® chips

yellow crinkle gift bag paper

small wooden ice cream spoons

markers

felt

scissors

glue

A Star of a Sandwich Snack

Ingredients:

bread

lunch meat or spread to make sandwiches

knife

paper plates

grapes or other small fruit

TOASTED STARS SNACK

Ingredients:

bread

cheese slices

star-shaped cookie cutter

cookie sheet

spatula

BEANBAG TOSS GAME

Supplies:

masking tape

three beanbags

posterboard and scissors (optional)

WHERE, OH WHERE, COULD THAT BABY BE? GAME

Supplies:

shallow box

hay, straw, or gift bag crinkle paper

baby doll

flashlight

or some other special treat in the center of the star. **Say: God made a promise to the people long ago that Jesus would be born. God kept that promise and then put a star in the sky so the wise men could find Jesus.**

Toasted Stars

Use a star-shaped cookie cutter to cut both bread and cheese into stars. Place the cheese on top of the bread and put them on a cookie sheet. Place the sheet into the oven. Set the oven to broil and watch the bread closely. It will toast quickly. Remove the toast from the pan with a spatula. Cool slightly and serve. The children can eat the bread and cheese scraps, or the bread scraps can be taken outside for the birds.

Say: God made a promise to the people long ago that Jesus would be born. God kept that promise and then put a star in the sky so the wise men could find Jesus.

GAMES:
Beanbag Toss

Use masking tape to make a large star on the floor, or cut a large star from posterboard and place it on the floor. Use masking tape to make a line for the children to stand behind. Give a child three beanbags and see if he or she can toss the beanbags onto the star. Remind the children that God promised long ago that Jesus would be born. God kept that promise and then put a bright star in the sky so the people could find Jesus.

Where, Oh Where, Could That Baby Be?

Before class, find a shallow box without a lid. Add some hay, straw, or crinkle paper to the box and place a baby doll on top. Hide the baby in the box somewhere in the room. Turn out the lights. Have the children look for the baby like the wise men did. When the baby doll is found, let the child who found it use a flashlight and shine it on the baby for all to see. Remind the children that God promised a long time ago that Jesus would be born and God kept that promise! **Say: After Jesus was born, God put a bright star in the sky so the wise men could find Jesus.**

SONG:

Use the tune "This Old Man" for the following words. Remind the children that a "promise" means that you will do what you said. **Say: God made a promise and kept the promise.**

What I said,

I will do.

That's a promise from me to you.

The words I said are really, really true.

That's a promise from me to you.

What God said,

God will do.

That's a promise from God to you.

The words God said are really, really true.

That's a promise from God to you.

PRAYER:

Pray: Dear God, thank you for keeping your promise. Baby Jesus was born just like you said he would be. Thank you for baby Jesus. Amen.

STEPPING STONES OF FAITH: GOD MADE THE WORLD & GOD MADE ME

"You (God) created me and put me together."
(Psalm 119:73, CEV)

STEPPING INTO THE BIBLE: Creation

(Genesis 1:1–2:22; Psalm 119:73)

In addition to involving the children in the story below by repeating a certain phrase, have some simple pictures showing each of these things that God made. For the picture of the child, a simple stick figure is great. Retell the story and let a child choose the appropriate picture from the stack.

Start the story by reading Genesis 1:1 from a Bible.

Say: "In the beginning, God created the heavens and the earth" (Genesis 1:1).

That means that God made the whole world.

God also made the daytime, and God made the nighttime.

God looked at everything made,

"And it was good!" (Have the children repeat this phrase and say it each time it is used in the story.)

Say: God made the sky, and God made the sea.

God made the land for you and for me.

God looked at everything made,

Let the children *say this part: And it was good!*

Say: **God made the plants, the sun, the moon, and the stars.**

God made all the fish that live in the sea.

God made the birds that sit in the trees.

God looked at everything made,

The children *say: And it was good!*

Say: **Then one day God made the animals.**

What are some animals you like to see?

Let the children name some favorite animals.

Say: **When all that was done, God made people.**

God looked at everything made,

The children *say: And it was good!)*

Again read from a Bible to the children. **Say: The Bible tells us God "created me and put me together"** (Psalm 119:73).

That means God made YOU!

God looked at everything made . . .

Everyone together: ***AND IT WAS GOOD!***

CRAFTS:
Making Me

Let each child decorate a paper plate to look like her or him. Talk about how many eyes they have and what color they are. Add a nose and a smile on the face. Cut ears from construction paper in skin tones for the child to add to each side of the head. What color hair does the child have? Glue on yarn pieces or gift bag crinkle paper in a color to match her or his hair. **Tell the child: God made you and put you together. God looked at everything made, and it was good!**

Put Me Together

Use the patterns on page 58 and pieces of construction paper to cut out a yellow hat, a tan or manila colored circle, and the body, arm, and leg pieces in any color for each child. Vary the colors to make the picture colorful. Help each child assemble the parts to put a scarecrow together. The large wedge is the scarecrow's body. The four smaller ones are the arms and legs. Glue the pieces to a whole sheet of paper. The child can then use markers to draw buttons on the scarecrow body. Put glue at the ends of the arms and legs and have the child add straw or gift bag crinkle paper to finish the scarecrow. Title the paper: "God Created Me and Put Me Together." (Psalm 119:73, CEV).

MAKING ME CRAFT Supplies:

inexpensive paper plates

crayons or markers

construction paper in skin tones

scissors

yarn pieces or gift bag crinkle paper in hair colors

glue

PUT ME TOGETHER CRAFT Supplies:

construction paper in various colors

scarecrow patterns (page 58)

scissors

glue

markers

straw or yellow gift bag crinkle paper

KiD KOOKiES Snack

Ingredients:

round sugar cookies

cake decorating tube

frosting

small candies, chocolate chips, or colorful cereal pieces

thin licorice

ME MUFFinS Snack

Ingredients:

paper plates

English muffins

cream cheese or other flavorful spread

plastic knives or wooden craft sticks

raisins or cereal pieces

miniature carrot sticks

shredded cheese

God Created Me and Put Me Together. (Psalm 119:73, CEV)

straw hat

face

Use Pattern pieces to assemble scarecrow.

strips for arms and legs

large rectangle for body

glue "straw" under arms and legs

All is assembled on 9×12-inch construction paper.

Snacks:
Kid Kookies

Give each child a large round sugar cookie. Use frosting in a decorating tube as "glue" to hold candies in place for the eyes and nose. Add a strip of thin licorice for a smile. Provide frosting in several colors for the hair. The cookies do not have to look like the child—just any happy kid will do! God made them all!

ME Muffins

If the idea of making a "Kid Kookie" without all the sugar is appealing, try making a "ME Muffin" instead. Let each child spread cream cheese or another flavorful spread on one-half of an open English muffin. Attach raisins or cereal pieces for facial features. A miniature carrot stick makes a great nose. Place the English muffin on a plate. Sprinkle shredded cheese around the top for hair.

Games:
Pin the Nose on the Smiley Face

Cut a large circle from posterboard. Draw two big eyes and a big smile on the face to make a smiley face to hang on the wall. Cut a smaller circle for each child from construction paper. These will be the noses. Curl a piece of tape for the back of each nose. Blindfold the child and see if she or he can put the nose in the right place on the smiley face. Some children do not like to be blindfolded—another option is to use dark sunglasses instead. Yes, they can see, but it's fun just the same! Remind the children that God made us and put us together—from our smiling faces all the way down to our toes!

Body Buddies

Pair each child with a buddy. If there is an odd number of children, the teacher can be a buddy. Tell the children that you will name a body part. If you **say: arms,** the children should touch their arms to the buddy's arms. If you **say: head,** the two buddies should touch heads. (Encourage them to do so gently.) Remind the children that God made our arms and legs and ears and hands and heads (and everything else). **Say: God made us and put us together.**

Song:

Use the tune to the first part of "You Are My Sunshine" for these words and add the motions as the song is sung:

God made the sunshine.

(Raise arms over your head and touch fingers together.)

God made the trees.

(Wave arms over head like a tree blowing in the wind.)

God made the rainbow,

(Draw a rainbow arc with your finger in the air.)

And God made me!

(Point to self.)

(Repeat the words and motions.)

Prayer:

Pray: **Dear God, you made everything there is! You made the whole world, and you made me. That's amazing! Thank you, God. I love you, God. Amen.**

Pin the Nose on the Smiley Face Game Supplies:

colored posterboard

scissors

marker

construction paper

tape

blindfold or dark sunglasses

Body Buddies Game Supplies:

Pattern: Put Me Together

The children will assemble the body parts and build a scarecrow. They will then add straw or crinkle paper at the ends of the arms and legs to make it look more like a scarecrow.

straw hat

head

body

leg   arm   arm   leg

STEPPING STONES OF FAITH:
GOD IS GOOD

"Shout praises to the LORD! He is good to us, and his love never fails." *(Psalm 107:1, CEV)*

STEPPING INTO THE BIBLE:
Hannah Has a Baby

(1 Samuel 1:6-20; 2:18-21)

Before class, trace the robe pattern (page 62) onto white construction paper. Make enough so that each child will have one to decorate later. Cut these out as the story is told. The robe is a simple "T" shape that is easy to cut.

Say: Hannah was married, but she did not have any children. She really wanted to have a baby. One day, Hannah went to worship God. She was feeling very sad. She prayed to God. She said, "I am so sad. Please let me have a baby boy."

The priest at the temple was named Eli. He did not hear what Hannah said when she prayed. Hannah prayed quietly. She prayed for a long time. When she got up, Eli talked to her. Hannah told him that she was talking to God about why she was so sad.

Eli told her she should go home and stop worrying. God was good. Eli was sure that God would answer her prayer. Eli did not know that Hannah was praying for a baby.

It was not long before Hannah found out she was going to have a baby. She was very happy! When her baby was born, it was a little boy. She named him Samuel.

When Samuel was a bit older, he went to the temple and stayed there. He helped Eli do his work at the temple. Every year his mother, Hannah, would travel to the temple to worship God. She made new clothes for Samuel and brought those to him.

Eli was happy that Samuel stayed at the temple to help him. Whenever he saw Samuel's mother and father, he would pray that God would bless them with more children. God was good to Hannah. Hannah did have more children. She had three more boys and two girls.

CRAFTS:
New Clothes

Say: Hannah's son, Samuel, lived and worked in the temple with Eli. Hannah made new clothes for him every year and took them to him. Have the children decorate the robes that were cut during the story. They can use crayons and markers to make Samuel's clothes as nice as they can be. Encourage them to add stripes and polka dots and zigzags for decorations.

Say: God was good to Hannah. God gave Hannah had a baby boy. Her boy grew up to be a good helper in the temple.

My Happy Handbook

Draw a large happy face on a sheet of construction paper turned sideways. This will be the book cover. Add four sheets of white paper behind the cover and staple the pages together to make a booklet. Title the first page "My Family." Title the second page "My Food," and the third page "My Friends." Leave the fourth page blank.

Remind the children that they can thank God for all these gifts. The children can draw the appropriate pictures for each page. Let each child think of something else that shows God is good. Have him or her draw that on the fourth page. Write what the child says it is on that page. Another way to make the booklet is to cut around the happy face on the cover and make all the pages in the booklet round like the cover. Then title the pages inside.

SNACKS:
Baby in a Blanket

Place a tortilla flat on the table. Place a pretzel rod in the center. Squeeze Cheez-Whiz® beside the pretzel. Wrap the tortilla around the pretzel rod much like a blanket is wrapped around a baby.

Baby Food

Collect and clean baby food jars. Put applesauce in each one and serve for a snack. Have the children think they are really eating baby food for a snack!

Say: Hannah really wanted a baby. Hannah prayed for a baby. She had a baby boy and named him Samuel.

NEW CLOTHES CRAFT Supplies:

robe patterns cut out earlier

crayons or markers

MY HAPPY HANDBOOK CRAFT Supplies:

construction paper

white paper

crayons or markers

stapler

BABY in a BLANKET Snack Ingredients:

tortillas

pretzel rods

Cheez-Whiz®

Games:
Baby Bag Memory Game

Place five or six baby items inside a baby bag. Pull them out one at a time and show them to the children. Be sure they know what each item is called. Now put all the items back in the bag. Pull out all but one of the items, and place them in front of the children. Can they tell you which item stayed in the bag?

Remind the children that Hannah really wanted a baby. **Say: Hannah prayed for a baby, and soon Samuel was born.**

Hannah Had a Baby

Use the following chant with the children. They can all pretend to rock a baby in their arms as they repeat this:

Hannah had a baby, a baby, a baby.

Hannah had a baby,

And the baby did this.

Show something the baby did, and have the children repeat it. Have the baby cry, suck a thumb, rub his eyes, smile, giggle, or coo. Let the children take turns being the leader and deciding what the baby will do.

Song:

Use the tune "Mary Had a Little Lamb" for these words:

God is really <u>good</u> to me,

<u>Good</u> to me, <u>good</u> to me.

God is really <u>good</u> to me.

Thank you, thank you, God!

Have the children stomp each time they sing the word "good." Repeat the song several times and change the action each time—they can clap, blink their eyes, twist their bodies, and so on.

Prayer:

Pray: Dear God, thank you for being so <u>good</u> to all of us. We love you. Amen.

BABY FOOD SNACK

Ingredients:

baby food jars

applesauce

spoons

BABY BAG MEMORY GAME

Supplies:

baby bag

baby items such as a rattle, a diaper, powder, a baby toy, baby wipes, and a baby bottle

HANNAH HAD A BABY GAME

Supplies:

Pattern: *New Clothes*

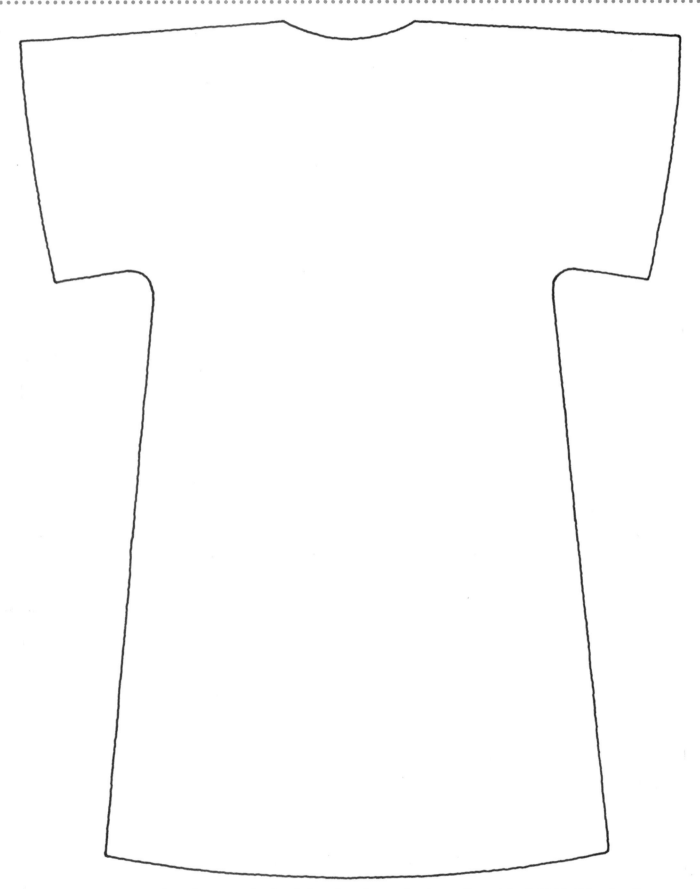

Stepping Stones of Faith:
GOD Will Never Stop Loving Me

"O give thanks to the God of heaven, for his steadfast love endures forever." *(Psalm 136:26, NRSV)*

Stepping Into the Bible:
The Forgiving Father
(Luke 15:11-24)

Invite the children to join in making the movements during the story. Briefly retell the story by using the motions again.

Say: Listening. Listening. (Cup hands to ears as if listening closely.)

Crowds of people followed Jesus wherever he went. They wanted to listen to Jesus. One day Jesus told the people a story. His story was about a man who had two sons. The younger son wanted to leave home. He asked his Dad for his share of the family money.

Walking. Walking. (Use right fingers to walk down left arm.)

The father gave his son the money. The older son stayed home and helped his dad, but the younger son packed his things and walked away. He walked far away from home. Soon all his money was gone. He had spent all of it. He had no money and no food to eat either. He walked some more because he needed to find a job.

Looking. Looking. (Put hand over eyebrows as if looking for something.)

He was looking and looking for a job. The only job he could find was taking care of someone's pigs. What a dirty job! He was so hungry—he wished he could eat what the pigs were eating! But no one gave him food to eat.

Thinking. Thinking. (Scratch head as if thinking hard.)

One day, the son decided to go back home. "I know my Dad will be unhappy with me. He will not like what I have done. I am so sad that I wasted all of that money. I will tell him I am sorry."

Running. Running. (Stand up and run in place.)

The son headed home. From a long way off, his father saw him coming. What a happy day! His son was coming home! He ran to see him, and he gave his son a big hug. The son told his father that he was sorry. He said, "I don't even deserve to be called your son anymore."

Cheering. Cheering. (Clap and cheer "Hooray!")

The father was not angry at his son. He called his helpers and said, "Good news! My son is home! Bring him some new clothes to wear. Bring a ring for his finger and sandals for his feet! We're going to have a party for him!"

The father was not angry after all.

Listening. Listening. (Cup hand to ear as if listening closely.)

When Jesus told the people a story, they listened to him. That was his way of teaching them about God. Jesus wanted the people to see that God is like this father. God loves us. Sometimes we may not do the right thing, but God loves us anyway. God will never stop loving you!

CRAFTS:
String Art

Before the children arrive, draw a circle in the center of a sheet of construction paper. Photocopy the rhyme about the string (page 68) so that each child will have a copy. For each child, cut a length of string or colorful yarn that is just long enough to go around the circle.

Give each child a photocopy of the rhyme. Help the child draw on top of the circle with a bottle of glue. Place the yarn on top of the glue. The string will want to stick to the child's fingers, so if you would like, help the child use a straw to place the string rather than the child using her or his fingers.

Read the rhyme about the string to the child as she or he glues it onto the paper:

STRING ART CRAFT Supplies:

construction paper

marker

string rhyme
(page 68)

yarn or string

scissors

glue

straws (optional)

heart-shaped
sponges

paint

shallow pan

There's something funny about this string.

It looks like a circle. It looks like a ring.

The circle keeps going, and it does not end.

That's how God loves me and all my friends.

Remind the child that God's love is like this circle. It never ends. It keeps going and going. **Say: God will never stop loving you.** Let the child then dip a heart-shaped sponge into a shallow pan of paint and print hearts all over the construction paper you prepared earlier.

Old CD, New Pig

Trace around an old CD or CD-ROM onto a piece of pink construction paper folded in half. Cut out the two pink circles for each child.

Have the child glue a pink circle to the front of the CD. Glue two large wiggle eyes on the face. Give each child a pink nut cup to make the pig's nose. Have the child color two nostrils on the bottom of the cup. Run a line of glue around the top of the nut cup and glue it to the center of the CD. (If you do not have pink nut cups, cut a paper towel roll into one-inch pieces. Wrap a one-inch-wide strip of pink paper around it. Then cut a circle large enough to cover the end of the tube. Color the nostrils on this part and glue it to the end of the tube. Now run a line of glue around the open end and press this pig's nose to the middle of the CD.) Use a marker to draw a smile on the pig's face.

Give the child the other pink circle and have her or him glue it to the back of the CD. Cut two small pink hearts for each child. Have the child glue the hearts upside down to the back of the pig for ears. The pointed ends stick up.

old CDs or CD-ROMs

pink construction paper

pencil

scissors

glue

large wiggle eyes

pink paper nut cups or paper towel rolls

black or red marker

pink chenille stems

tape

paper plates, pink paint, and paintbrushes (optional)

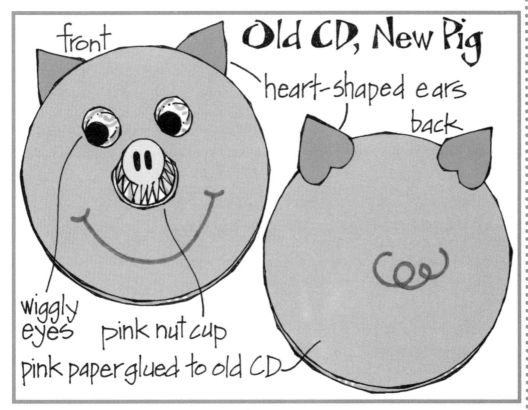

front

Old CD, New Pig

heart-shaped ears

back

wiggly eyes

pink nut cup

pink paper glued to old CD

Wrap a pink chenille stem around a pencil to make a curly pig's tail. Slide it off the pencil and tape one end of it to the back of the CD.

If there are not enough CDs, use paper plates. Let the child color or paint the plate pink. Add the eyes, nose, mouth, and tail as described.

Remind the children that the brother lived with the pigs and took care of them after he left his father.

snacks:
Heart Pancakes

Prepare pancake batter as directed on the package. Divide the batter into two bowls. Tint one bowl of batter pink by adding a few drops of red food coloring. Cook round pancakes as usual. Some will be brown, and some will be dark pink. Use a heart-shaped cookie cutter to cut a heart from the center of a brown pancake. Do the same to a pink pancake. Put the brown heart in the pink pancake and put the pink heart in the brown pancake. Add syrup and give each child a fork. As the children eat their pancakes, remind them that God loves them and that God will never stop loving them.

Ice Cream Sundaes

Serve each child a bowl of ice cream. Let her or him top the ice cream with sprinkles and gummy hearts. As the children eat their ice cream, ask them what happens to their ice cream if it stays out of the cold refrigerator too long. *(It melts.)* **Ask: What happens to gummy hearts?** *(They stay the same.)* **Say: The gummy hearts remind us of God's love. God's love always stays with us.**

Games:
Pigs in the Pen

Spread the children out around the room and have them sit on the floor. Walk among them. Explain to the children that you will tap a child on the head and name an animal. That child then has to stand up and make the sound that animal makes. The children must listen carefully, though, because you might **say: pig.** When you **say: pig,** all of the children have to stand up and oink like a pig. Move rapidly among the children to keep the game interesting.

As the game ends, remind the children of the story they heard about the son who left home. He worked taking care of pigs when he ran out of money. His father did not stay mad at him for what he did. **Say: God is like that father. God does not stay mad at us when we do something wrong.**

Hugs and More Hugs

Start the game by reminding the children that God loves us. In fact, God will never stop loving us! When we love someone, we like to give them a hug. Have the children spread out around the room and remain standing as they play this hugging game.

Start as the leader and then let a child take your place. This game is guaranteed to get silly! Call out something or someone for the children to hug. End the game by having them all come and give YOU a hug! Great for fun and giggles. Here are some suggested hugs:

Hug your foot.

Hug your belly.

Hug one person.

Hug a toy.

Hug two people.

Hug your head.

Hug your lips.

Hug yourself.

Hug ME!

SONG:

Use the tune "Clementine" for these words. Add motions to the song to get the children involved. Here are some suggestions to try:

- Shake your head "no" when you sing the word "never."

- Hold up your hand as a policeman would when you say "stop."

- Hug yourself when you say "loving."

God will never,

God will never,

Never **STOP** loving me.

God will never,

God will never,

Never **STOP** loving me.

PRAYER:

Pray: Dear God, I am glad you love me. And I am really glad that you will never stop loving me. Amen.

PIGS IN THE PEN GAME Supplies:

HUGS AND MORE HUGS GAME Supplies:

There's something
funny about this string.

It looks like a circle.

It looks like a ring.

The circle keeps going,
and it does not end.

That's how God loves me
and all my friends.

ALL ABOUT ME

Child's Name _____

Parent's or Guardian's Name(s) _____

_____

Child's Address _____

City _____ **State** _____ **Zip Code** _____

Telephone Number _____

Parent's or Guardian's Cell Phone Number _____

Child's Birthday _____

Allergies or Situations the Teacher Should Know About _____

_____

_____

Where Will the Parent or Guardian Be While the Child Is in Session? _____

_____

_____